The Gospel of John

THE
NEW INTERNATIONAL VERSION

The Bible Society

Copyright © 1974 by
the New York Bible Society International
Printed in Great Britain
English—NIV John
BFBS—1980—15M—NIV 560
ISBN 0 564 06861 6

Printed by Gospel Press, South Molton, Devon

JOHN

The Word Became Flesh

1 In the beginning was the Word, and the Word was with God, and the Word was God. ² He was with God in the beginning.

³ Through him all things were made; without him nothing was made that has been made. ⁴ In him was life, and that life was the light of men. ⁵ The light shines in the darkness, but the darkness has not understood*ᵃ* it.

⁶ There came a man who was sent from God; his name was John. ⁷ He came as a witness to testify concerning that light, so that through him all men might believe. ⁸ He himself was not the light; he came only as a witness to the light. ⁹ The true light that gives light to every man was coming into the world.*ᵇ*

¹⁰ He was in the world, and though the world was made through him, the world did not recognize him. ¹¹ He came to that which was his own, but his own did not receive him. ¹² Yet to all who received him, to those who believed in his name, he gave the right to become children of God—¹³ children born not of natural descent,*ᶜ* nor of human decision or a husband's will, but born of God.

¹⁴ The Word became flesh and lived for a while among us. We have seen his glory, the glory of the one and only [Son],*ᵈ* who came from the Father, full of grace and truth.

¹⁵ John testifies concerning him. He cries out, saying, "This was he of whom I said, 'He who comes after me has surpassed me because he was before me.' " ¹⁶ From

ᵃ 5 Or *overpowered*
ᵇ 9 Or *This was the true light that gives light to every man who comes into the world.*
ᶜ 13 Greek *of bloods*   *ᵈ* 14 Or *the Only Begotten*

1

the fullness of his grace we have all received one blessing after another. ¹⁷ For the law was given through Moses; grace and truth came through Jesus Christ. ¹⁸ No man has ever seen God, but God the only*e* [Son],*f* who is at the Father's side, has made him known.

John the Baptist Denies Being the Christ

¹⁹ Now this was John's testimony when the Jews of Jerusalem sent priests and Levites to ask him who he was. ²⁰ He did not fail to confess, but confessed freely, "I am not the Christ.*g*"

²¹ They asked him, "Then who are you? Are you Elijah?"

He said, "I am not."

"Are you the Prophet?"

He answered, "No."

²² Finally they said, "Who are you? Give us an answer to take back to those who sent us. What do you say about yourself?"

²³ John replied in the words of Isaiah the prophet, "I am the voice of one calling in the desert, 'Make straight the way for the Lord.' "*h*

²⁴ Now some Pharisees who had been sent ²⁵ questioned him, "Why then do you baptize if you are not the Christ,*i* nor Elijah, nor the Prophet?"

²⁶ "I baptize with*j* water," John replied, "but among you stands one you do not know. ²⁷ He is the one who comes after me, the thongs of whose sandals I am not worthy to untie."

²⁸ This all happened at Bethany on the other side of the Jordan, where John was baptizing.

Jesus the Lamb of God

²⁹ The next day John saw Jesus coming toward him and said, "Look, the Lamb of God, who takes away the sin of

---

e 18 Or *but God the only begotten*
f 18 Some MSS read *but the only Son* (or *but the only begotten Son*).
g 20 Or *Messiah.* "The Christ" (Greek) and "the Messiah" (Hebrew) both mean "the Anointed One."
h 23 Isaiah 40:3   *i* 25 Or *Messiah*   *j* 26, Or *in*

the world! [30] This is the one I meant when I said, 'A man who comes after me has surpassed me because he was before me.' [31] I myself did not know him but the reason I came baptizing with[k] water was that he might be revealed to Israel."

[32] Then John gave this testimony: "I saw the Spirit come down from heaven as a dove and remain on him. [33] I would not have known him, except that the one who sent me to baptize with[k] water told me, 'The man on whom you see the Spirit come down and remain is he who will baptize with the Holy Spirit.' [34] I have seen and I testify that this is the Son of God."

Jesus' First Disciples

[35] The next day John was there again with two of his disciples. [36] When he saw Jesus passing by, he said, "Look, the Lamb of God!"

[37] When the two disciples heard him say this, they followed Jesus. [38] Turning around, Jesus saw them following and asked, "What do you want?"

They said, "Rabbi" (which means Teacher), "where are you staying?"

[39] "Come," he replied, "and you will see."

So they went and saw where he was staying, and spent that day with him. It was about the tenth hour.

[40] Andrew, Simon Peter's brother, was one of the two who heard what John had said and who had followed Jesus. [41] The first thing Andrew did was to find his brother Simon and tell him, "We have found the Messiah" (that is, the Christ).

[42] Then he brought Simon to Jesus, who looked at him and said, "You are Simon, the son of John. You will be called Cephas" (which, when translated, is Peter[l]).

Jesus Calls Philip and Nathanael

[43] The next day Jesus decided to leave for Galilee. Finding Philip, he said to him, "Follow me."

[44] Philip, like Andrew and Peter, was from the town of

[k] 31, 33 Or *in*
[l] 42 Both *Cephas* (Aramaic) and *Peter* (Greek) mean *rock.*

Bethsaida. ⁴⁵ Philip found Nathanael and told him, "We have found the one Moses wrote about in the Law, and about whom the prophets also wrote—Jesus of Nazareth, the son of Joseph."

⁴⁶ "Nazareth! Can anything good come from there?" Nathanael asked.

"Come and see," said Philip.

⁴⁷ When Jesus saw Nathanael approaching, he said of him, "Here is a true Israelite, in whom there is nothing false."

⁴⁸ "How do you know me?" Nathanael asked.

Jesus answered, "I saw you while you were still under the fig tree before Philip called you."

⁴⁹ Then Nathanael declared, "Rabbi, you are the Son of God; you are the King of Israel."

⁵⁰ Jesus said, "You believe*ᵐ* because I told you I saw you under the fig tree. You shall see greater things than that." ⁵¹ He then added, "I tell you the truth, you shall all see heaven open, and the angels of God ascending and descending on the Son of Man."

Jesus Changes Water to Wine

2 On the third day a wedding took place at Cana in Galilee. Jesus' mother was there, ² and Jesus and his disciples had also been invited to the wedding. ³ When the wine was gone, Jesus' mother said to him, "They have no more wine."

⁴ "Why do you involve me?*ᵃ*" Jesus replied, "My time has not yet come."

⁵ His mother said to the servants, "Do whatever he tells you."

⁶ Nearby stood six stone water jars, the kind used by the Jews for ceremonial washing, each holding from seventeen to twenty-five gallons.

⁷ Jesus said to the servants, "Fill the jars with water"; so they filled them to the brim.

⁸ Then he told them, "Now draw some out and take it to the master of the banquet."

ᵐ 50 Or *Do you believe . . .?*
ᵃ 4 Greek *involve me, woman* (a polite form of address)

4

They did so, [9] and the master of the banquet tasted the water that had been turned into wine. He did not realize where it had come from, though the servants who had drawn the water knew. Then he called the bridegroom aside [10] and said, "Everyone brings out the choice wine first and then the cheaper wine after the guests have had too much to drink; but you have saved the best till now."

[11] This, the first of his miraculous signs, Jesus performed in Cana of Galilee. He thus revealed his glory, and his disciples put their faith in him.

Jesus Clears the Temple

[12] After this he went down to Capernaum with his mother and brothers and his disciples. Here they stayed for a few days.

[13] When it was almost time for the Jewish Passover, Jesus went up to Jerusalem. [14] In the temple court he found men selling cattle, sheep and doves, and others sitting at tables exchanging money. [15] So he made a whip out of cords, and drove all from the temple area, both sheep and cattle; he scattered the coins of the moneychangers and overturned their tables. [16] To those who sold doves, he said, "Get these out of here! How dare you turn my Father's house into a market!"

[17] His disciples remembered that it is written, "Zeal for your house will consume me."[b]

[18] Then the Jews demanded of him, "What miraculous sign can you show us to prove your authority to do all this?"

[19] Jesus answered them, "Destroy this temple, and I will raise it again in three days."

[20] The Jews replied, "It has taken forty-six years to build this temple, and you are going to raise it in three days?" [21] But the temple he had spoken of was his body. [22] After he was raised from the dead, his disciples recalled what he had said. Then they believed the Scripture and the words that Jesus had spoken.

[23] Now while he was in Jerusalem at the Passover Feast,

[b] 17 Psalm 69:9

many people saw the miraculous signs he was doing and trusted in his name.*c* *24* But Jesus would not entrust himself to them, for he knew all men. *25* He did not need man's testimony about man, for he knew what was in a man.

Jesus Teaches Nicodemus

3 Now there was a man of the Pharisees named Nicodemus, a member of the Jewish ruling council. *2* He came to Jesus at night and said, "Rabbi, we know you are a teacher who has come from God. For no one could perform the miraculous signs you are doing if God were not with him."

3 In reply Jesus declared, "I tell you the truth, unless a man is born again,*a* he cannot see the kingdom of God."

4 "But," said Nicodemus, "how can a man be born when he is old? Surely he cannot enter a second time into his mother's womb to be born!"

5 Jesus answered, "I tell you the truth, unless a man is born of water and the Spirit, he cannot enter the kingdom of God. *6* Flesh gives birth to flesh, but the Spirit*b* gives birth to spirit. *7* You should not be surprised at my saying, 'You*c* must be born again.'*d* *8* The wind blows wherever it pleases. You may hear its sound, but you cannot tell where it comes from or where it is going. So it is with everyone born of the Spirit."

9 "How can this be?" Nicodemus asked.

10 "You are a teacher of Israel," said Jesus, "and do you not understand these things? *11* I tell you the truth, we speak of what we know, and we testify to what we have seen, but still you people do not accept our testimony. *12* I have spoken to you of earthly things and you do not believe; how then will you believe if I speak of heavenly things? *13* No one has ever gone into heaven except the one who came from heaven—the Son of Man. *14* Just as Moses lifted up the snake in the desert, so the Son of Man must be lifted

c 23 Or *and put their trust in him*
a 3 Or *born from above*   *b* 6 Or *but spirit*
c 7 The Greek is plural.   *d* 7 Or *born from above*

up, [15] that everyone who believes may have eternal life in him.[e]

[16] "For God so loved the world that he gave his one and only Son,[f] that whoever believes in him shall not perish but have everlasting life. [17] For God did not send his Son into the world to condemn the world, but to save the world through him. [18] Whoever believes in him is not condemned, but whoever does not believe stands condemned already because he has not believed in the name of God's one and only Son.[g] [19] This is the verdict: Light has come into the world, but men loved darkness instead of light because their deeds were evil. [20] Everyone who does evil hates the light, and will not come into the light for fear that his deeds will be exposed. [21] But whoever lives by the truth comes into the light, so that it may be seen plainly that what he has done has been done through God."[h]

John the Baptist's Testimony about Jesus

[22] After this, Jesus and his disciples went out into the Judean countryside, where he spent some time with them, and baptized. [23] Now John also was baptizing at Aenon near Salim, because there was plenty of water, and people were constantly coming to be baptized. [24] (This was before John was put in prison.) [25] An argument developed between some of John's disciples and a certain Jew over the matter of ceremonial washing. [26] They came to John and said to him, "Rabbi, that man who was with you on the other side of the Jordan—the one about whom you testified—well, he is baptizing, and everyone is going to him."

[27] To this John replied, "A man can receive only what is given him from heaven. [28] You yourselves can testify that I said, 'I am not the Christ[i] but am sent ahead of him.' [29] The bride belongs to the bridegroom. The friend who attends the bridegroom waits and listens for him, and is full of joy when he hears the bridegroom's voice. That joy is

[e] 15 Or *believes in him may have eternal life*
[f] 16 Or *his only begotten Son*   [g] 18 Or *God's only begotten Son*
[h] 21 Some interpreters end the quotation after verse 15.
[i] 28 Or *Messiah*

mine, and it is now complete. [30] He must become greater; I must become less important.

[31] "The one who comes from above is above all; the one who is from the earth belongs to the earth, and speaks as one from the earth. The one who comes from heaven is above all. [32] He testifies to what he has seen and heard, but no one accepts his testimony. [33] The man who has accepted it has certified that God is truthful. [34] For the one whom God has sent speaks the words of God; to him God gives the Spirit without limit. [35] The Father loves the Son and has placed everything in his hands. [36] Whoever puts his faith in the Son has eternal life, but whoever rejects the Son will not see that life, for God's wrath remains on him."

Jesus Talks with a Samaritan Woman

4 The Pharisees heard that Jesus was gaining and baptizing more disciples than John, [2] although in fact it was not Jesus who baptized, but his disciples. [3] When the Lord learned of this, he left Judea and went back once more to Galilee.

[4] Now he had to go through Samaria. [5] So he came to a town in Samaria called Sychar, near the plot of ground Jacob had given to his son Joseph. [6] Jacob's well was there, and Jesus, tired as he was from the journey, sat down by the well. It was about the sixth hour.

[7] When a Samaritan woman came to draw water, Jesus said to her, "Will you give me a drink?" [8] (His disciples had gone into the town to buy food.)

[9] The Samaritan woman said to him, "You are a Jew and I am a Samaritan woman. How can you ask me for a drink?" (For Jews do not associate with Samaritans.[a])

[10] Jesus answered her, "If you knew the gift of God and who it is that asks you for a drink, you would have asked him and he would have given you living water."

[11] "Sir," the woman said, "you have nothing to draw with and the well is deep. Where can you get this living water? [12] Are you greater than our father Jacob, who gave

[a] 9 Or *do not use dishes Samaritans have used*

8

us the well and drank from it himself, as did also his sons and his flocks and herds?"

¹³ Jesus answered, "Everyone who drinks this water will be thirsty again, ¹⁴ but whoever drinks the water I give him will never thirst. Indeed, the water I give him will become in him a spring of water welling up to everlasting life."

¹⁵ The woman said to him, "Sir, give me this water so that I won't get thirsty and have to keep coming here to draw water."

¹⁶ He told her, "Go, call your husband and come back."

¹⁷ "I have no husband," she replied.

Jesus said to her, "You are right when you say you have no husband. ¹⁸ The fact is, you have had five husbands, and the man you now have is not your husband. What you have just said is quite true."

¹⁹ "Sir," the woman said, "I can see that you are a prophet. ²⁰ Our fathers worshipped on this mountain, but you Jews claim that the place where we must worship is in Jerusalem."

²¹ Jesus declared, "Believe me, woman, a time is coming when you will worship the Father neither on this mountain nor in Jerusalem. ²² You Samaritans worship what you do not know; we worship what we do know, for salvation is from the Jews. ²³ Yet a time is coming and has now come when the true worshippers will worship the Father in spirit and truth, for they are the kind of worshippers the Father seeks. ²⁴ God is spirit, and his worshippers must worship in spirit and in truth."

²⁵ The woman said, "I know that Messiah" (called Christ) "is coming. When he comes, he will explain everything to us."

²⁶ Then Jesus declared, "I who speak to you am he."

The Disciples Rejoin Jesus

²⁷ Just then his disciples returned and were surprised to find him talking with a woman. But no one asked, "What do you want?" or "Why are you talking with her?"

²⁸ Then, leaving her water jar, the woman went back to the town and said to the people, ²⁹ "Come, see a man who

told me everything I ever did. Could this be the Christ?"[b]
³⁰ They came out of the town and made their way toward him.

³¹ Meanwhile his disciples urged him, "Rabbi, eat something."

³² But he said to them, "I have food to eat that you know nothing about."

³³ Then his disciples said to each other, "Could someone have brought him food?"

³⁴ "My food," said Jesus, "is to do the will of him who sent me and to finish his work. ³⁵ Do you not say, 'Four months more and then the harvest'? I tell you, open your eyes and look at the fields! They are ripe for harvest. ³⁶ Even now the reaper draws his wages, even now he harvests the crop for eternal life, so that the sower and the reaper may be glad together. ³⁷ Thus the saying 'One sows and another reaps' is true. ³⁸ I sent you to reap what you have not worked for. Others have done the hard work, and you have reaped the benefits of their labour."

Many Samaritans Believe

³⁹ Many of the Samaritans from that town believed in him because of the woman's testimony, "He told me everything I ever did." ⁴⁰ So when the Samaritans came to him, they urged him to stay with them, and he stayed two days. ⁴¹ And because of his words many more became believers.

⁴² They said to the woman, "We no longer believe just because of what you said; now we have heard for ourselves, and we know that this man really is the Saviour of the world."

Jesus Heals the Official's Son

⁴³ After the two days he left for Galilee. ⁴⁴ (Now Jesus himself had pointed out that a prophet has no honour in his own country.) ⁴⁵ When he arrived in Galilee, the Galileans welcomed him. They had seen all that he had done in Jerusalem at the Passover Feast, for they also had been there.

⁴⁶ Once more he visited Cana in Galilee, where he had turned the water into wine. And there was a certain royal

[b] 29 Or *Messiah*

official whose son lay sick at Capernaum. ⁴⁷ When this man heard that Jesus had arrived in Galilee from Judea, he went to him and begged him to come and heal his son, who was close to death.

⁴⁸ "Unless you people see miraculous signs and wonders," Jesus told him, "you will never believe."

⁴⁹ The royal official said, "Sir, come down before my child dies."

⁵⁰ Jesus replied, "You may go. Your son will live."

The man took Jesus at his word and departed. ⁵¹ While he was still on the way, his servants met him with the news that his boy was living. ⁵² When he inquired as to the time when his son had got better, they said to him, "The fever left him yesterday at the seventh hour."

⁵³ Then the father realized that this was the exact time at which Jesus had said to him, "Your son will live." So he and all his household believed.

⁵⁴ This was the second miraculous sign that Jesus performed, having come from Judea to Galilee.

The Healing at the Pool

5 Some time later, Jesus went up to Jerusalem for a feast of the Jews. ² Now there is in Jerusalem near the Sheep Gate a pool, which in Aramaic is called Bethesda*ᵃ* and which is surrounded by five covered colonnades. ³ Here a great number of disabled people used to lie—the blind, the lame, the paralysed.*ᵇ* ⁵ One who was there had been an invalid for thirty-eight years. ⁶ When Jesus saw him lying there and learned that he had been in this condition for a long time, he asked him, "Do you want to get well?"

⁷ "Sir," the invalid replied, "I have no one to help me into the pool when the water is stirred. While I am trying to get in, someone else goes down ahead of me."

⁸ Then Jesus said to him, "Get up! Pick up your mat and

ᵃ 2 Some early MSS read *Bethzatha*; others *Bethsaida*.
ᵇ 3 Some MSS—*and they waited for the moving of the waters*. Some less important MSS also add verse 4: *From time to time an angel of the Lord would come down and stir up the waters. The first one into the pool after each such disturbance would be cured of whatever disease he had.*

walk." ⁹ At once the man was cured; he picked up his mat and walked.

The day on which this took place was a Sabbath, ¹⁰ and so the Jews said to the man who had been healed, "It is the Sabbath; the law forbids you to carry your mat."

¹¹ But he replied, "The man who made me well said to me, 'Pick up your mat and walk.'"

¹² So they asked him, "Who is this fellow who told you to pick it up and walk?"

¹³ The man who was healed had no idea who it was, for Jesus had slipped away in the crowd.

¹⁴ Later Jesus found him at the temple and said to him, "See, you are well again. Stop sinning or something worse may happen to you." ¹⁵ The man went away and told the Jews that it was Jesus who had made him well.

Life through the Son

¹⁶ So, because Jesus was doing these things on the Sabbath, the Jews persecuted him. ¹⁷ Jesus said to them, "My Father is always at his work to this very day, and I, too, am working." ¹⁸ For this reason the Jews tried all the harder to kill him; not only was he breaking the Sabbath, but he was even calling God his own Father, making himself equal with God.

¹⁹ Jesus gave them this answer: "I tell you the truth, the Son can do nothing by himself; he can do only what he sees his Father doing, because whatever the Father does the Son also does. ²⁰ For the Father loves the Son and shows him all he does. Yes, to your amazement he will show him even greater things than these. ²¹ For just as the Father raises the dead and gives them life, even so the Son gives life to whom he is pleased to give it. ²² Moreover, the Father judges no one, but has entrusted all judgment to the Son, ²³ that all may honour the Son just as they honour the Father. He who does not honour the Son does not honour the Father who sent him.

²⁴ "I tell you the truth, whoever hears my word and believes him who sent me has eternal life and will not be condemned; he has crossed over from death to life. ²⁵ I tell

you the truth, a time is coming and has now come when the dead will hear the voice of the Son of God and those who hear will live. [26] For as the Father has life in himself, so he has granted the Son to have life in himself. [27] And he has given him authority to judge because he is the Son of Man.

[28] "Do not be amazed at this, for a time is coming when all who are in their graves will hear his voice [29] and come out—those who have done good will rise to live, and those who have done evil will rise to be condemned. [30] By myself I can do nothing; I judge only as I hear, and my judgment is just, for I seek not to please myself but him who sent me.

Testimonies about Jesus

[31] "If I testify about myself, my testimony is not valid. [32] There is another who testifies in my favour, and I know that his testimony about me is valid.

[33] "You have sent to John and he has testified to the truth. [34] Not that I accept human testimony; but I mention it that you may be saved. [35] John was a lamp that burned and gave light, and you chose for a time to enjoy his light.

[36] "I have testimony weightier than that of John. For the very work that the Father has given me to finish, and which I am doing, testifies that the Father has sent me. [37] And the Father who sent me has himself testified concerning me. You have never heard his voice nor seen his form, [38] nor does his word dwell in you, for you do not believe the one he sent. [39] You diligently study[c] the Scriptures because you think that by them you possess eternal life. These are the Scriptures that testify about me, [40] yet you refuse to come to me to have life.

[41] "I do not accept praise from men, [42] but I know you. I know that you do not have God's love in your hearts. [43] I have come in my Father's name, and you do not accept me; but if someone else comes in his own name, you will accept him. [44] How can you believe if you accept praise from one another, yet make no effort to obtain the praise that comes from the only God?[d]

[c] 39 Or *Study diligently* (the imperative)
[d] 44 Some early MSS read *the Only One.*

⁴⁵ "But do not think I will accuse you before the Father. Your accuser is Moses, on whom your hopes are set. ⁴⁶ If you believed Moses, you would believe me, for he wrote about me. ⁴⁷ But since you do not believe what he wrote, how are you going to believe what I say?"

Jesus Feeds the Five Thousand

6 Some time after this, Jesus crossed to the far shore of the Sea of Galilee (that is, the Sea of Tiberias), ² and a great crowd of people followed him because they saw the miraculous signs he had performed on the sick. ³ Then Jesus went up on the hillside and sat down with his disciples. ⁴ The Jewish Passover Feast was near.

⁵ When Jesus looked up and saw a great crowd coming toward him, he said to Philip, "Where shall we buy bread for these people to eat?" ⁶ He asked this only to test him, for he already had in mind what he was going to do.

⁷ Philip answered him, "Eight months' wages*ᵃ* would not buy enough bread for each one to have a bite!"

⁸ Another of his disciples, Andrew, Simon Peter's brother, spoke up, ⁹ "Here is a boy with five small barley loaves and two small fish, but how far will they go among so many?"

¹⁰ Jesus said, "Have the people sit down." There was plenty of grass in that place, and the men sat down, about five thousand of them. ¹¹ Jesus then took the loaves, gave thanks, and distributed to those who were seated as much as they wanted. He did the same with the fish.

¹² When they had all had enough to eat, he said to his disciples, "Gather the pieces that are left over. Let nothing be wasted." ¹³ So they gathered them and filled twelve baskets with the pieces of the five barley loaves left over by those who had eaten.

¹⁴ After the people saw the miraculous sign that Jesus did, they began to say: "Surely this is the Prophet who is to come into the world." ¹⁵ Jesus, knowing that they intended to come and make him king by force, withdrew again into the hills by himself.

ᵃ 7 Greek *200 denarii*

Jesus Walks on the Water

[16] When evening came, his disciples went down to the lake, [17] where they got into a boat and set off across the lake for Capernaum. By now it was dark, and Jesus had not yet joined them. [18] A strong wind was blowing and the waters grew rough. [19] When they had rowed three or four miles, they saw Jesus approaching the boat, walking on the water; and they were terrified. [20] But he said to them, "It is I; don't be afraid." [21] Then they were willing to take him into the boat, and immediately the boat reached the shore where they were heading.

[22] The next day the crowd that had stayed on the opposite shore of the lake realized that only one boat had been there, and that Jesus had not entered it with his disciples, but that they had gone away alone. [23] Then some boats from Tiberias landed near the place where the people had eaten the bread after the Lord had given thanks. [24] Once the crowd realized that neither Jesus nor his disciples were there, they got into the boats and went to Capernaum in search of Jesus.

Jesus the Bread of Life

[25] When they found him on the other side of the lake, they asked him, "Rabbi, when did you get here?"

[26] Jesus answered, "I tell you the truth, you are looking for me, not because you saw miraculous signs but because you ate the loaves and had your fill. [27] Do not work for food that spoils, but for food that endures to eternal life, which the Son of Man will give you. On him God the Father has placed his seal of approval."

[28] Then they asked him, "What must we do to do the work of God?"

[29] Jesus answered, "The work of God is this: to believe in the one whom he has sent."

[30] So they asked him, "What miraculous sign then will you give that we may see it and believe you? What will you do? [31] Our forefathers ate the manna in the desert; as it is written, 'He gave them bread from heaven to eat.' "[b]

[b] 31 Exodus 16:4; Psalm 78:24

[32] Jesus said to them, "I tell you the truth, it is not Moses who has given you the bread from heaven, but it is my Father who gives you the true bread from heaven. [33] For the bread of God is he who comes down from heaven and gives life to the world."

[34] "Sir," they said, "from now on give us this bread."

[35] Then Jesus declared, "I am the bread of life. He who comes to me will never go hungry, and he who believes in me will never be thirsty. [36] But as I told you, you have seen me and still you do not believe. [37] All that the Father gives me will come to me, and whoever comes to me I will never drive away. [38] For I have come down from heaven not to do my will but to do the will of him who sent me. [39] And this is the will of him who sent me, that I shall lose none of all that he has given me, but raise them up at the last day. [40] For my Father's will is that everyone who looks to the Son and believes in him shall have eternal life, and I will raise him up at the last day."

[41] At this the Jews began to murmur against him because he said, "I am the bread that came down from heaven." [42] They said, "Is this not Jesus, the son of Joseph, whose father and mother we know? How can he now say, 'I came down from heaven'?"

[43] "Stop murmuring among yourselves," Jesus answered. [44] "No one can come to me unless the Father who sent me draws him, and I will raise him up at the last day. [45] It is written in the Prophets, 'They will all be taught by God.'[c] Everyone who listens to the Father and learns from him comes to me. [46] No one has seen the Father except the one who is from God; only he has seen the Father. [47] I tell you the truth, he who believes has everlasting life. [48] I am the bread of life. [49] Your forefathers ate the manna in the desert, yet they died. [50] But there is the bread that comes down from heaven, which a man may eat and not die. [51] I am the living bread that came down from heaven. If a man eats of this bread, he will live for ever. This bread is my flesh, which I will give for the life of the world."

[c] 45 Isaiah 54:13

⁵² Then the Jews began to argue sharply among themselves, "How can this man give us his flesh to eat?"

⁵³ Jesus said to them, "I tell you the truth, unless you eat the flesh of the Son of Man and drink his blood, you have no life in you. ⁵⁴ Whoever eats my flesh and drinks my blood has eternal life, and I will raise him up at the last day. ⁵⁵ For my flesh is real food and my blood is real drink. ⁵⁶ Whoever eats my flesh and drinks my blood remains in me, and I in him. ⁵⁷ Just as the living Father sent me and I live because of the Father, so the one who feeds on me will live because of me. ⁵⁸ This is the bread that came down from heaven. Our forefathers ate [manna] and died, but he who feeds on this bread will live for ever." ⁵⁹ He said this while teaching in the synagogue in Capernaum.

Many Disciples Desert Jesus

⁶⁰ On hearing it many of his disciples said, "This is a hard teaching. Who can accept it?"

⁶¹ Aware that his disciples were grumbling about this, Jesus said to them, "Does this offend you? ⁶² What if you see the Son of Man ascend to where he was before! ⁶³ The Spirit gives life; the flesh counts for nothing. The words I have spoken to you are spirit*d* and they are life. ⁶⁴ Yet there are some of you who do not believe." For Jesus had known from the beginning which of them did not believe and who would betray him. ⁶⁵ He went on to say, "This is why I told you that no one can come to me unless the Father has enabled him."

⁶⁶ From this time many of his disciples turned back and no longer followed him.

⁶⁷ "Do you want to leave too?" Jesus asked the Twelve.

⁶⁸ Simon Peter answered him, "Lord, to whom shall we go? You have the words of eternal life. ⁶⁹ We believe and know that you are the Holy One of God."

⁷⁰ Then Jesus replied, "Have I not chosen you, the Twelve? Yet one of you is a devil!" ⁷¹ (He meant Judas, the son of Simon Iscariot, who, though one of the Twelve, was later to betray him.)

d 63 Or *Spirit*

17

Jesus Goes to the Feast of Tabernacles

7 After this, Jesus went around in Galilee, purposely staying away from Judea because the Jews there were waiting to take his life. ² But when the Jewish Feast of Tabernacles was near, ³ Jesus' brothers said to him, "You ought to leave here and go to Judea, so that your disciples may see the miracles you do. ⁴ No one who wants to become a public figure acts in secret. Since you are doing these things, show yourself to the world." ⁵ For even his own brothers did not believe in him.

⁶ Therefore Jesus told them, "The right time for me has not yet come; for you any time is right. ⁷ The world cannot hate you, but it hates me because I testify that what it does is evil. ⁸ You go to the Feast. I am not yet going up to this Feast,ᵃ because for me the right time has not yet come." ⁹ Having said this, he stayed in Galilee.

¹⁰ However, after his brothers had left for the Feast, he went also, not publicly, but in secret. ¹¹ Now at the Feast the Jews were watching for him and asking, "Where is that man?"

¹² Among the crowds there was widespread whispering about him. Some said, "He is a good man."

Others replied, "No, he deceives the people." ¹³ But no one would say anything publicly about him for fear of the Jews.

Jesus Teaches at the Feast

¹⁴ Not until halfway through the Feast did Jesus go up to the temple court and begin to teach. ¹⁵ The Jews were amazed and asked, "How did this man get such learning without having studied?"

¹⁶ Jesus answered, "My teaching is not my own. It comes from him who sent me. ¹⁷ If a man chooses to do God's will, he will find out whether my teaching comes from God or whether I speak on my own. ¹⁸ He who speaks on his own does so to gain honour for himself, but he who works for the honour of the one who sent him is a man of truth; there

ᵃ 8 Some early MSS omit *yet*.

is nothing false about him. [19] Has not Moses given you the law? Yet not one of you keeps the law. Why are you trying to kill me?"

[20] "You are demon-possessed," the crowd answered. "Who is trying to kill you?"

[21] Jesus said to them, "I did one miracle, and you are all astonished. [22] Yet, because Moses gave you circumcision (though actually it did not come from Moses, but from the patriarchs), you circumcise a child on the Sabbath. [23] Now if a child can be circumcised on the Sabbath so that the law of Moses may not be broken, why are you angry with me for healing the whole man on the Sabbath? [24] Stop judging by mere appearances, and make a right judgment."

Is Jesus the Christ?

[25] At that point some of the people of Jerusalem began to ask, "Isn't this the man they are trying to kill?[26] Here he is, speaking publicly, and they are not saying a word to him. Have the authorities really concluded that he is the Christ?[b] [27] But we know where this man is from; when the Christ[b] comes, no one will know where he is from."

[28] Then Jesus, still teaching in the temple court, cried out, "Yes, you know me, and you know where I am from. I am not here on my own, but he who sent me is true. You do not know him, [29] but I know him because I am from him and he sent me."

[30] At this they tried to seize him, but no one laid a hand on him, because his time had not yet come. [31] Still, many in the crowd put their faith in him. They said, "When the Christ[b] comes, will he do more miraculous signs than this man?"

[32] The Pharisees heard the crowd whispering such things about him. Then the chief priests and the Pharisees sent temple guards to arrest him.

[33] Jesus said, "I am with you for only a short time, and then I go to the one who sent me. [34] You will look for me, but you will not find me; and where I am, you cannot come."

[35] The Jews said to one another, "Where does this man

[b] 26, 27, 31 Or *Messiah*

intend to go that we cannot find him? Will he go where our people live scattered among the Greeks, and teach the Greeks? ³⁶ What did he mean when he said, 'You will look for me, but you will not find me,' and 'Where I am, you cannot come'?"

³⁷ On the last and greatest day of the Feast, Jesus stood and said in a loud voice, "If a man is thirsty, let him come to me and drink. ³⁸ Whoever believes in me,ᶜ as the Scripture has said, streams of living water will flow from within him." ³⁹ By this he meant the Spirit, whom those who believed in him were later to receive. Up to that time the Spirit had not been given, since Jesus had not yet been glorified.

⁴⁰ On hearing his words, some of the people said, "Surely this man is the Prophet."

⁴¹ Others said, "He is the Christ."ᵈ

Still others asked, "How can the Christᵈ come from Galilee? ⁴² Does not the Scripture say that the Christᵈ will come from David's familyᵉ and from Bethlehem, the town where David lived?" ⁴³ Thus the people were divided because of Jesus. ⁴⁴ Some wanted to seize him, but no one laid a hand on him.

Unbelief of the Jewish Leaders

⁴⁵ Finally the temple guards went back to the chief priests and Pharisees, who asked them, "Why didn't you bring him in?"

⁴⁶ "No one ever spoke the way this man does," the guards declared.

⁴⁷ "You mean he has deceived you also?" the Pharisees retorted. ⁴⁸ "Has any of the rulers or of the Pharisees put his trust in him? ⁴⁹ No! But this mob that knows nothing of the law—there is a curse on them."

⁵⁰ Nicodemus, who had gone to Jesus earlier and who was one of their own number, asked, ⁵¹ "Does our law con-

---

ᶜ 38 Or *If a man is thirsty,*
    let him come to me.
    And let him drink,
    who believes in me.
ᵈ 41, 42 Or *Messiah*   ᵉ 42 Greek *seed*

demn a man without first hearing him to find out what he is doing?"

⁵² They replied, "Are you from Galilee, too? Look into it, and you will find that a prophet*ᶠ* does not come out of Galilee."

[The most reliable early manuscripts omit John 7:53–8:11]

⁵³ Then they all left, each to his own home.

The Woman Caught in Adultery

8 But Jesus went to the Mount of Olives. ² At dawn he appeared again in the temple court, where all the people gathered around him, and he sat down to teach them. ³ The teachers of the law and the Pharisees brought in a woman caught in adultery. They made her stand before the group and ⁴ said to Jesus, "Teacher, this woman was caught in the act of adultery. ⁵ In the Law Moses commanded us to stone such women. Now what do you say?" ⁶ They were using this question as a trap, in order to have a basis for accusing him.

But Jesus bent down and started to write on the ground with his finger. ⁷ When they kept on questioning him, he straightened up and said to them, "If any one of you is without sin, let him begin stoning her." ⁸ Again he stooped down and wrote on the ground.

⁹ At this, those who heard began to go away one at a time, the older ones first, until only Jesus was left, with the woman still standing there. ¹⁰ Jesus straightened up and asked her, "Woman, where are they? Has no one condemned you?"

¹¹ "No one, sir," she said.

"Then neither do I condemn you," Jesus declared. "Go now and leave your life of sin."

The Validity of Jesus' Testimony

¹² When Jesus spoke again to the people, he said, "I am the light of the world. Whoever follows me will never walk in darkness, but will have the light of life."

ᶠ 52 Or the Prophet

21

¹³ The Pharisees challenged him, "Here you are, appearing as your own witness; your testimony is not valid."

¹⁴ Jesus answered, "Even if I testify on my own behalf, my testimony is valid, for I know where I came from and where I am going. But you have no idea where I come from or where I am going. ¹⁵ You judge by human standards; I pass judgment on no one. ¹⁶ But if I do judge, my decisions are right, because I am not alone. I stand with the Father who sent me. ¹⁷ In your own Law it is written that the testimony of two men is valid. ¹⁸ I am one who testifies for myself; my other witness is the one who sent me—the Father."

¹⁹ Then they asked him, "Where is your father?"

"You do not know me or my Father," Jesus replied. "If you knew me, you would know my Father also." ²⁰ He spoke these words while teaching in the temple area near the place where the offerings were put. Yet no one seized him, because his time had not yet come.

²¹ Once more Jesus said to them, "I am going away, and you will look for me, and you will die in your sin. Where I go, you cannot come."

²² This made the Jews ask, "Will he kill himself? Is that why he says, 'Where I go, you cannot come'?"

²³ But he continued, "You are from below; I am from above. You are of this world; I am not of this world. ²⁴ I told you that you would die in your sins; if you do not believe that I am [the one I claim to be][a], you will indeed die in your sins."

²⁵ "Who are you, anyway?" they asked.

"Just what I have been claiming all along," Jesus replied. ²⁶ "I have much to say in judgment of you. But he who sent me is reliable, and what I have heard from him I tell the world."

²⁷ They did not understand that he was telling them about his Father. ²⁸ So Jesus said, "When you have lifted up the Son of Man, then you will know who I am[b] and that I do nothing on my own but speak just what the Father has taught me. ²⁹ The one who sent me is with me; he has not

[a] 24 Or *I am He*   [b] 28 Or *know that I am he*

left me alone, for I always do what pleases him." ³⁰ Even as he spoke, many put their faith in him.

The Children of Abraham

³¹ To the Jews who had believed him, Jesus said, "If you hold to my teaching, you are really my disciples. ³² Then you will know the truth, and the truth will set you free."

³³ They answered him, "We are Abraham's descendants*c* and have never been slaves of anyone. How can you say that we shall be set free?"

³⁴ Jesus replied, "I tell you the truth, everyone who sins is a slave to sin. ³⁵ Now a slave has no permanent place in the family, but a son belongs to it for ever. ³⁶ So if the Son sets you free, you will be free indeed. ³⁷ I know you are Abraham's descendants.*c* Yet you are ready to kill me, because you have no room for my word. ³⁸ I am telling you what I have seen in the Father's presence, and you do what you have heard from your father."*d*

³⁹ "Abraham is our father," they answered.

"If you were Abraham's children," said Jesus, "then you would do the things Abraham did.*e* ⁴⁰ As it is, you are determined to kill me, a man who has told you the truth that I heard from God. Abraham did not do such things. ⁴¹ You are doing the things your own father does."

"We are not illegitimate children," they protested. "The only Father we have is God himself."

The Children of the Devil

⁴² Jesus said to them, "If God were your Father, you would love me, for I came from God and now am here. I have not come on my own; but he sent me. ⁴³ Why is my language not clear to you? Because you are unable to hear what I say. ⁴⁴ You belong to your father, the devil, and you want to carry out your father's desire. He was a murderer from the beginning, not holding to the truth, for there is no truth in him. When he lies, he speaks his native language,

c 33, 37 Greek *seed*
d 38 Or *presence. Therefore do what you have heard from the Father.*
e 39 Some early MSS read *then do the things Abraham did.*

for he is a liar and the father of lies. [45] Yet because I tell the truth, you do not believe me! [46] Can any of you prove me guilty of sin? If I am telling the truth, why don't you believe me? [47] He who belongs to God hears what God says. The reason you do not hear is that you do not belong to God."

The Claims of Jesus about Himself

[48] The Jews answered him, "Aren't we right in saying that you are a Samaritan and demon-possessed?"

[49] "I am not possessed by a demon," said Jesus, "but I honour my Father and you dishonour me. [50] I am not seeking glory for myself; but there is one who seeks it, and he is the judge. [51] I tell you the truth, if a man keeps my word, he will never see death."

[52] At this the Jews exclaimed, "Now we know that you are demon-possessed! Abraham died and so did the prophets, yet you say that if a man keeps your word, he will never taste death. [53] Are you greater than our father Abraham? He died, and so did the prophets. Who do you think you are?"

[54] Jesus replied, "If I glorify myself, my glory means nothing. My Father, whom you claim as your God, is the one who glorifies me. [55] Though you do not know him, I know him. If I said I did not, I would be a liar like you, but I do know him and keep his word. [56] Your father Abraham rejoiced at the thought of seeing my day; he saw it and was glad."

[57] "You are not yet fifty years old," the Jews said to him, "and you have seen Abraham!"

[58] "I tell you the truth," Jesus answered, "before Abraham was born, I am!" [59] At this, they picked up stones to stone him, but Jesus hid himself, slipping away from the temple grounds.

Jesus Heals a Man Born Blind

9 As he went along, he saw a man blind from birth. [2] His disciples asked him, "Rabbi, who sinned, this man or his parents, that he was born blind?"

³ "Neither this man nor his parents sinned," said Jesus, "but this happened so that the work of God might be displayed in his life. ⁴ As long as it is day, we must do the work of him who sent me. Night is coming, when no one can work. ⁵ While I am in the world, I am the light of the world."

⁶ Having said this, he spat on the ground, made some mud with the saliva, and put it on the man's eyes. ⁷ "Go," he told him, "wash in the pool of Siloam" (this word means Sent). So the man went and washed, and came home seeing.

⁸ His neighbours and those who had formerly seen him begging asked, "Isn't this the same man who used to sit and beg?" ⁹ Some claimed that he was.

Others said, "No, he only looks like him."

But he himself insisted, "I am the man."

¹⁰ "How then were your eyes opened?" they demanded.

¹¹ He replied, "The man they call Jesus made some mud and put it on my eyes. He told me to go to Siloam and wash. So I went and washed, and then I could see."

¹² "Where is this man?" they asked him.

"I don't know," he said.

The Pharisees Investigate the Healing

¹³ They brought to the Pharisees the man who had been blind. ¹⁴ Now the day on which Jesus had made the mud and opened the man's eyes was a Sabbath. ¹⁵ Therefore the Pharisees also asked him how he had received his sight. "He put mud on my eyes," the man replied, "and I washed, and now I see."

¹⁶ Some of the Pharisees said, "This man is not from God, for he does not keep the Sabbath."

But others asked, "How can a sinner do such miraculous signs?" So they were divided.

¹⁷ Finally they turned again to the blind man, "What have you to say about him? It was your eyes he opened."

The man replied, "He is a prophet."

¹⁸ The Jews still did not believe that he had been blind and had received his sight until they sent for the man's parents. ¹⁹ "Is this your son?" they asked. "Is this the one you say was born blind? How is it that now he can see?"

²⁰ "We know he is our son," the parents answered, "and we know he was born blind. ²¹ But how he can see now, or who opened his eyes, we don't know. Ask him. He is of age; he will speak for himself." ²² His parents said this because they were afraid of the Jews, for already the Jews had decided that anyone who acknowledged that Jesus was the Christ[a] would be put out of the synagogue. ²³ That was why his parents said, "He is of age; ask him."

²⁴ A second time they summoned the man who had been blind. "Give glory to God,"[b] they said. "We know this man is a sinner."

²⁵ He replied, "Whether he is a sinner or not, I don't know. One thing I do know: I was blind but now I see!"

²⁶ Then they asked him, "What did he do to you? How did he open your eyes?"

²⁷ He answered, "I have told you already and you did not listen. Why do you want to hear it again? Do you want to become his disciples, too?"

²⁸ Then they hurled insults at him and said, "You are this fellow's disciple! We are disciples of Moses! ²⁹ We know that God spoke to Moses, but as for this fellow, we don't even know where he comes from."

³⁰ The man answered, "Now that is remarkable! You don't know where he comes from, yet he opened my eyes. ³¹ We know that God does not listen to sinners. He listens to the godly man who does his will. ³² Nobody has ever heard of opening the eyes of a man born blind. ³³ If this man were not from God, he could do nothing."

³⁴ To this they replied, "You were steeped in sin at birth; how dare you lecture us!" And they threw him out.

Spiritual Blindness

³⁵ Jesus heard that they had thrown him out, and when he found him, he said, "Do you believe in the Son of Man?"

³⁶ "Who is he, sir?" the man asked. "Tell me so that I may believe in him."

[a] 22 That is, *the Messiah*
[b] 24 A solemn charge to tell the truth (see Joshua 7:19).

³⁷ Jesus said, "You have now seen him; in fact, he is the one speaking with you."

³⁸ Then the man said, "Lord, I believe," and he worshipped him.

³⁹ Jesus said, "For judgment I have come into this world, so that the blind will see and those who see will turn out to be blind."

⁴⁰ Some Pharisees who were with him heard him say this and asked, "What? Are we blind too?"

⁴¹ Jesus said, "If you were blind, you would not be guilty of sin; but now that you claim you can see, your guilt remains.

The Shepherd and His Flock

10 "I tell you the truth, the man who does not enter the sheep pen by the gate, but climbs in by some other way, is a thief and a robber. ² The man who enters by the gate is the shepherd of his sheep. ³ The watchman opens the gate for him, and the sheep listen to his voice. He calls his own sheep by name and leads them out. ⁴ When he has brought out all his own, he goes on ahead of them, and his sheep follow him because they know his voice. ⁵ But they will never follow a stranger; in fact, they will run away from him because they do not recognize a stranger's voice." ⁶ Jesus used this figure of speech, but they did not understand what he was telling them.

⁷ Therefore Jesus said again, "I tell you the truth, I am the gate for the sheep. ⁸ All who ever came before me were thieves and robbers, but the sheep did not listen to them. ⁹ I am the gate; whoever enters through me will be saved.^a He will come in and go out, and find pasture. ¹⁰ The thief comes only to steal and kill and destroy; I have come that they may have life, and have it to the full.

¹¹ "I am the good shepherd. The good shepherd lays down his life for the sheep. ¹² The hired hand is not the shepherd who owns the sheep. So when he sees the wolf coming, he abandons the sheep and runs away. Then the wolf attacks the flock and scatters it. ¹³ The man runs away

^a 9 Or *kept safe*

because he is a hired hand and cares nothing for the sheep.

¹⁴ "I am the good shepherd; I know my sheep and my sheep know me—¹⁵ Just as the Father knows me and I know the Father—and I lay down my life for the sheep. ¹⁶ I have other sheep that are not of this flock. I must bring them also. They too will listen to my voice, and there shall be one flock and one shepherd. ¹⁷ The reason my Father loves me is that I lay down my life—only to take it up again. ¹⁸ No one takes it from me, but I lay it down of my own accord. I have authority to lay it down and authority to take it up again. This command I received from my Father."

¹⁹ At these words the Jews were again divided. ²⁰ Many of them said, "He is demon-possessed and raving mad. Why listen to him?"

²¹ But others said, "These are not the sayings of a man possessed by a demon. How can a demon open the eyes of the blind?"

The Unbelief of the Jews

²² Then came the Feast of Dedication[b] at Jerusalem. It was winter, ²³ and Jesus was in the temple area walking in Solomon's Colonnade. ²⁴ The Jews gathered around him, saying, "How long will you keep us in suspense? If you are the Christ,[c] tell us plainly."

²⁵ Jesus answered, "I did tell you, but you do not believe. The miracles I do in my Father's name speak for me, ²⁶ but you do not believe because you do not belong to my flock. ²⁷ My sheep listen to my voice; I know them, and they follow me. ²⁸ I give them eternal life, and they shall never perish; no one can snatch them out of my hand. ²⁹ My Father, who has given them to me, is greater than all;[d] no one can snatch them out of my Father's hand. ³⁰ I and the Father are one."

³¹ Again the Jews picked up stones to stone him, ³² but Jesus said to them, "I have shown you many great miracles from the Father. For which of these do you stone me?"

---

b 22 That is, *Hanukkah*   *c* 24 Or *Messiah*
d 29 Many early MSS read *What my Father has given me is greater than all.*

³³ "We are not stoning you for any of these," replied the Jews, "but for blasphemy, because you, a mere man, claim to be God."

³⁴ Jesus answered them, "Is it not written in your Law, 'I have said you are gods'?ᵉ ³⁵ If he called them 'gods,' to whom the word of God came—and the Scripture cannot be broken—³⁶ what about the one whom the Father set apart as his very own and sent into the world? Why then do you accuse me of blasphemy because I said, 'I am God's Son'? ³⁷ Do not believe me unless I do what my Father does. ³⁸ But if I do it, even though you do not believe me, believe the evidence of the miracles, that you may learn and understand that the Father is in me, and I in the Father." ³⁹ Again they tried to seize him, but he escaped their grasp.

⁴⁰ Then Jesus went back across the Jordan to the place where John had been baptizing in the early days. Here he stayed ⁴¹ and many people came to him. They said, "Though John never performed a miraculous sign, all that John said about this man was true." ⁴² And in that place many believed in Jesus.

The Death of Lazarus

11 Now a man named Lazarus was sick. He was from Bethany, the village of Mary and her sister Martha. ² This Mary, whose brother Lazarus now lay sick, was the same one who poured perfume on the Lord and wiped his feet with her hair. ³ So the sisters sent word to Jesus, "Lord, the one you love is sick."

⁴ When he heard this, Jesus said, "This sickness will not end in death. No, it is for God's glory so that God's Son may be glorified through it." ⁵ Jesus loved Martha and her sister and Lazarus. ⁶ Yet when he heard that Lazarus was sick, he stayed where he was two more days.

⁷ Then he said to his disciples, "Let us go back to Judea."

⁸ "But Rabbi," they said, "a short while ago the Jews tried to stone you, and yet you are going back there?"

⁹ Jesus answered, "Are there not twelve hours of daylight? A man who walks by day will not stumble, for he sees by

ᵉ 34 Psalm 82:6

this world's light. ¹⁰ It is when he walks by night that he stumbles, for he has no light."

¹¹ After he had said this, he went on to tell them, "Our friend Lazarus has fallen asleep; but I am going there to wake him up."

¹² His disciples replied, "Lord, if he sleeps, he will get better." ¹³ Jesus had been speaking of his death, but his disciples thought he meant natural sleep.

¹⁴ So then he told them plainly, "Lazarus is dead, ¹⁵ yet for your sake so that you may believe, I am glad I was not there. But let us go to him."

¹⁶ Then Thomas, called Didymus, said to the rest of the disciples, "Let us also go, that we may die with him."

Jesus Comforts the Sisters

¹⁷ On his arrival, Jesus found that Lazarus had already been in the tomb for four days. ¹⁸ Bethany was less than two miles from Jerusalem, ¹⁹ and many Jews had come to Martha and Mary to comfort them in the loss of their brother. ²⁰ When Martha heard that Jesus was coming, she went out to meet him, but Mary stayed at home.

²¹ "Lord," Martha said to Jesus, "if you had been here, my brother would not have died. ²² But I know that even now God will give you whatever you ask."

²³ Jesus said to her, "Your brother will rise again."

²⁴ Martha answered, "I know he will rise again in the resurrection at the last day."

²⁵ Jesus said to her, "I am the resurrection and the life. He who believes in me will live, even though he dies; ²⁶ and whoever lives and believes in me will never die. Do you believe this?"

²⁷ "Yes, Lord," she told him, "I believe that you are the Christ,^a the Son of God, who was to come into the world."

²⁸ And after she had said this, she went back and called her sister Mary aside. "The Teacher is here," she said, "and is asking for you." ²⁹ When Mary heard this, she got up quickly and went to him. ³⁰ Now Jesus had not yet entered the village, but was still at the place where Martha had met

^a 27 Or *Messiah*

him. [31] When the Jews who had been with Mary in the house, comforting her, noticed how quickly she got up and went out, they followed her, supposing she was going to the tomb to mourn there.

[32] When Mary reached the place where Jesus was and saw him, she fell at his feet and said, "Lord, if you had been here, my brother would not have died."

[33] When Jesus saw her weeping, and the Jews who had come along with her also weeping, he was deeply moved and troubled. [34] "Where have you laid him?" he asked.

"Come and see, Lord," they replied.

[35] Jesus wept.

[36] Then the Jews said, "See how he loved him!"

[37] But some of them said, "Could not he who opened the eyes of the blind man have kept this man from dying?"

Jesus Raises Lazarus from the Dead

[38] Jesus, once more deeply moved, came to the tomb. It was a cave with a stone laid across the entrance. [39] "Take away the stone," he said.

"But, Lord," said Martha, the sister of the dead man, "by this time there is a bad odour, for he has been there four days."

[40] Then Jesus said, "Did I not tell you that if you believed, you would see the glory of God?"

[41] So they took away the stone. Then Jesus looked up and said, "Father, I thank you that you have heard me. [42] I knew that you always hear me, but I said this for the benefit of the people standing here, that they may believe that you sent me."

[43] When he had said this, Jesus called in a loud voice, "Lazarus, come out!" [44] The dead man came out, his hands and feet wrapped with strips of linen, and a cloth around his face.

Jesus said to them, "Take off the grave clothes and let him go."

The Plot to Kill Jesus

[45] Therefore many of the Jews who had come to visit Mary, and had seen what Jesus did, put their faith in him.

31

⁴⁶ But some of them went to the Pharisees and told them what Jesus had done. ⁴⁷ Then the chief priests and the Pharisees called a meeting of the Sanhedrin.

"What are we accomplishing?" they asked. "Here is this man performing many miraculous signs. ⁴⁸ If we let him go on like this, everyone will put his trust in him, and then the Romans will come and take away both our place[b] and our nation."

⁴⁹ Then one of them, named Caiaphas, who was high priest that year, spoke up, "You know nothing at all! ⁵⁰ You do not realize that it is better for you that one man die for the people than that the whole nation perish."

⁵¹ He did not say this on his own, but as high priest that year he prophesied that Jesus would die for the Jewish nation, ⁵² and not only for that nation but also for the scattered children of God, to bring them together and make them one. ⁵³ So from that day on they plotted to take his life.

⁵⁴ Therefore Jesus no longer moved about publicly among the Jews. Instead he withdrew to a region near the desert, to a village called Ephraim, where he stayed with his disciples.

⁵⁵ When it was almost time for the Jewish Passover, many went up from the country to Jerusalem for their ceremonial cleansing before the Passover. ⁵⁶ They kept looking for Jesus, and as they stood in the temple area they asked one another, "What do you think? Isn't he coming to the Feast at all?" ⁵⁷ But the chief priests and Pharisees had given orders that if anyone found out where Jesus was, he should report it so that they might arrest him.

Jesus Anointed at Bethany

12 Six days before the Passover, Jesus arrived at Bethany, where Lazarus lived, whom Jesus had raised from the dead. ² Here a dinner was given in Jesus' honour. Martha served, while Lazarus was among those reclining at the table with him. ³ Then Mary took about a pint of pure nard, an expensive perfume; she poured it on Jesus' feet and wiped his feet with her hair. And the house was filled with the fragrance of the perfume.

[b] 48 Or *temple*

⁴ But one of his disciples, Judas Iscariot, who was later to betray him, objected, ⁵ "Why wasn't this perfume sold and the money given to the poor? It was worth a year's wages."ᵃ ⁶ He did not say this because he cared about the poor but because he was a thief; as keeper of the money, he used to help himself to what was put into it.

⁷ "Leave her alone," Jesus replied. "It was meant that she should save this perfume for the day of my burial. ⁸ You will always have the poor among you, but you will not always have me."

⁹ Meanwhile a large crowd of Jews found out that Jesus was there and came, not only because of him but also to see Lazarus, whom he had raised from the dead. ¹⁰ So the chief priests made plans to kill Lazarus as well, ¹¹ for on account of him many of the Jews were going over to Jesus and putting their faith in him.

The Triumphal Entry

¹² The next day the great crowd that had come for the Feast heard that Jesus was on his way to Jerusalem. ¹³ They took palm branches and went out to meet him, shouting,

"Hosanna!ᵇ

Blessed is he who comes in the name of the Lord!ᶜ

Blessed is the King of Israel!

¹⁴ Jesus found a young donkey and sat upon it, as Scripture says,

¹⁵ "Do not be afraid, O daughter of Zion;

see, your king is coming,

seated on a donkey's colt."ᵈ

¹⁶ At first his disciples did not understand all this. Only after Jesus was glorified did they realize that these things had been written about him and that they had done these things to him.

¹⁷ Now the crowd that was with him had continued to spread the word that he had called Lazarus from the tomb,

ᵃ 5 Greek *300 denarii*
ᵇ 13 A Hebrew expression meaning "Save!" which became an exclamation of praise.
ᶜ 13 Psalm 118:25, 26　　　ᵈ 15 Zech. 9:9

raising him from the dead.*e* [18] Many people, because they had heard that he had given this miraculous sign, went out to meet him. [19] So the Pharisees said to one another, "See, this is getting us nowhere. Look how the whole world has gone after him!"

Jesus Predicts His Death

[20] Now there were some Greeks among those who went up to worship at the Feast. [21] They came to Philip, who was from Bethsaida in Galilee, with a request. "Sir," they said, "we would like to see Jesus." [22] Philip went to tell Andrew; Andrew and Philip in turn told Jesus.

[23] Jesus replied, "The hour has come for the Son of Man to be glorified. [24] I tell you the truth, unless a kernel of wheat falls to the ground and dies, it remains only a single seed. But if it dies, it produces many seeds. [25] The man who loves his life will lose it, while the man who hates his life in this world will keep it for eternal life. [26] Whoever serves me must follow me; and where I am, my servant also will be. My Father will honour the one who serves me.

[27] "Now my heart is troubled, and what shall I say? 'Father, save me from this hour'? No, it was for this very reason I came to this hour. [28] Father, glorify your name!"

Then a voice came from heaven, "I have glorified it, and will glorify it again." [29] The crowd that was there and heard it said it had thundered; others said an angel had spoken to him.

[30] Jesus said, "This voice was for your benefit, not mine. [31] Now is the time for judgment on this world; now the prince of this world will be driven out. [32] But I, when I am lifted up from the earth, will draw all men to myself." [33] He said this to show the kind of death he was going to die.

[34] The crowd spoke up, "We have heard from the Law that the Christ*f* will remain for ever, so how can you say, 'The Son of Man must be lifted up?' Who is this 'Son of Man'?"

e 17 Or *Now the crowd that had been with him when he called Lazarus from the tomb and raised him from the dead were telling everyone.*
f 34 Or *Messiah*

³⁵ Then Jesus told them, "You are going to have the light just a little while longer. Walk while you have the light, before darkness overtakes you. The man who walks in the dark does not know where he is going. ³⁶ Put your trust in the light while you have it, so that you may become sons of light." When he had finished speaking, Jesus left and hid himself from them.

The Jews Continue in Their Unbelief

³⁷ Even after Jesus had done all these miraculous signs in their presence, they still would not believe in him. ³⁸ This was to fulfil the word of Isaiah the prophet:

"Lord, who has believed our message,
and to whom has the arm of the Lord been revealed?"*g*

³⁹ For this reason they could not believe, because, as Isaiah says elsewhere,

⁴⁰ "He has blinded their eyes
and deadened their hearts,
so they can neither see with their eyes,
nor understand with their hearts,
nor turn and I would heal them."*h*

⁴¹ Isaiah said this because he saw Jesus' glory, and spoke about him.

⁴² Yet at the same time many even among the leaders believed in him. But because of the Pharisees they would not confess their faith for fear they would be put out of the synagogue; ⁴³ for they loved praise from men more than praise from God.

⁴⁴ Then Jesus cried out, "When a man believes in me, he does not believe in me only, but in the one who sent me. ⁴⁵ When he looks at me, he sees the one who sent me. ⁴⁶ I have come into the world as a light, so that no one who believes in me should stay in darkness.

⁴⁷ "As for the person who hears my words but does not keep them, I do not judge him. For I did not come to judge the world, but to save it. ⁴⁸ There is a judge for the one who rejects me and does not accept my words; that very word

g 38 Isaiah 53:1   *h* 40 Isaiah 6:10

which I spoke will condemn him at the last day. [49] For I did not speak of my own accord, but the Father who sent me commanded me what to say and how to say it. [50] I know that his command leads to eternal life. So whatever I say is just what the Father has told me to say."

Jesus Washes His Disciples' Feet

13 It was just before the Passover Feast. Jesus knew that the time had come for him to leave this world and go to the Father. Having loved his own who were in the world, he now showed them the full extent of his love.

[2] The evening meal was being served, and the devil had already prompted Judas Iscariot, son of Simon, to betray Jesus. [3] Jesus knew that the Father had put all things under his power, and that he had come from God and was returning to God, [4] so he got up from the meal, took off his outer clothing, and wrapped a towel around his waist. [5] After that, he poured water into a basin and began to wash his disciples' feet, drying them with the towel that was wrapped around him.

[6] He came to Simon Peter, who said to him, "Lord, are you going to wash my feet?"

[7] Jesus replied, "You do not realize now what I am doing, but later you will understand."

[8] "No," said Peter, "you shall never wash my feet."

Jesus answered, "Unless I wash you, you have no part with me."

[9] "Then, Lord," Simon Peter replied, "not just my feet but my hands and my head as well!"

[10] Jesus answered, "A person who has had a bath needs only to wash his feet; his whole body is clean. And you are clean, though not every one of you." [11] For he knew who was going to betray him, and that was why he said not every one was clean.

[12] When he had finished washing their feet, he put on his clothes and returned to his place. "Do you understand what I have done for you?" he asked them. [13] "You call me 'Teacher' and 'Lord,' and rightly so, for that is what I am.

[14] Now that I, your Lord and Teacher, have washed your feet, you also should wash one another's feet. [15] I have set you an example that you should do as I have done for you. [16] I tell you the truth, no servant is greater than his master, nor is a messenger greater than the one who sent him. [17] Once you know these things, you will be blessed if you do them.

Jesus Predicts His Betrayal

[18] "I am not referring to all of you; I know those I have chosen. But this is to fulfil the scripture: 'He who shares my bread has lifted up his heel against me.'[a]

[19] "I am telling you now before it happens, so that when it does happen you will believe that I am He. [20] I tell you the truth, whoever accepts anyone I send accepts me; and whoever accepts me accepts the one who sent me."

[21] After he had said this, Jesus was deeply troubled and testified, "I tell you the truth, one of you is going to betray me."

[22] His disciples stared at one another, at a loss to know which of them he meant. [23] One of them, the disciple whom Jesus loved, was reclining next to him. [24] Simon Peter motioned to this disciple and said, "Ask him which one he means."

[25] Leaning back against Jesus, he asked him, "Lord, who is it?"

[26] Jesus answered, "It is the one to whom I will give this piece of bread when I have dipped it in the dish." Then, dipping the piece of bread, he gave it to Judas Iscariot, son of Simon. [27] As soon as Judas took the bread, Satan entered into him.

"What you are about to do, do quickly," Jesus told him, [28] but no one at the meal understood why Jesus said this to him. [29] Since Judas had charge of the money, some thought Jesus was telling him to buy what was needed for the Feast, or to give something to the poor. [30] As soon as Judas had taken the bread, he went out. And it was night.

[a] 18 Psalm 41:9

Jesus Predicts Peter's Denial

[31] When he was gone, Jesus said, "Now is the Son of Man glorified and God is glorified in him. [32] If God is glorified in him,[b] then God will glorify the Son in himself, and will glorify him at once.

[33] "My children, I will be with you only a little longer. You will look for me, and just as I told the Jews, so I tell you now: Where I am going, you cannot come.

[34] "A new commandment I give you: Love one another. As I have loved you, so you must love one another. [35] All men will know that you are my disciples if you love one another."

[36] Simon Peter asked him, "Lord, where are you going?"

Jesus replied, "Where I am going, you cannot follow now, but you will follow later."

[37] Peter asked, "Lord, why can't I follow you now? I will lay down my life for you."

[38] Then Jesus answered, "Will you really lay down your life for me? I tell you the truth, before the cock crows, you will disown me three times!

Jesus Comforts His Disciples

14 "Do not let your hearts be troubled. Trust in God;[a] trust also in me. [2] There are many rooms in my Father's house; otherwise, I would have told you. I am going there to prepare a place for you. [3] And if I go and prepare a place for you, I will come back and take you to be with me that you also may be where I am. [4] You know the way to the place where I am going."

Jesus the Way to the Father

[5] Thomas said to him, "Lord, we don't know where you are going, so how can we know the way?"

[6] Jesus answered, "I am the way—and the truth and the life. No one comes to the Father except through me. [7] If you really knew me, you would know[b] my Father as well. From now on, you do know him and have seen him."

[b] 32 Many early MSS omit *If God is glorified in him.*

[a] 1 Or *You trust in God*

[b] 7 Some early MSS read *If you really have known me, you will know.*

8 Philip said, "Lord, show us the Father and that will be enough for us."

9 Jesus answered, "Don't you know me, Philip, even after I have been among you such a long time? Anyone who has seen me has seen the Father. How can you say, "Show us the Father'? 10 Don't you believe that I am in the Father, and that the Father is in me? The words I say to you are not just my own. Rather, it is the Father, living in me, who is doing his work. 11 Believe me when I say that I am in the Father and the Father is in me; or at least believe on the evidence of the miracles themselves. 12 I tell you the truth, anyone who has faith in me will do what I have been doing. He will do even greater things than these, because I am going to the Father. 13 And I will do whatever you ask in my name, so that the Son may bring glory to the Father. 14 You may ask me for anything in my name, and I will do it. 15 If you love me, you will do what I command.

Jesus Promises the Holy Spirit

16 "I will ask the Father, and he will give you another Counsellor, 17 the Spirit of truth, to be with you for ever. The world cannot accept this Counsellor, because it neither sees him nor knows him. But you know him, for he lives with you and will be in you. 18 I will not leave you as orphans; I will come to you. 19 Before long, the world will not see me any more, but you will see me. Because I live, you also will live. 20 On that day you will realize that I am in my Father, and you are in me, and I am in you. 21 Whoever has my commands and obeys them, he is the one who loves me. He who loves me will be loved by my Father, and I too will love him and show myself to him."

22 Then Judas (not Judas Iscariot) said, "But, Lord, why do you intend to show yourself to us and not to the world?"

23 Jesus replied, "If anyone loves me, he will obey my teaching. My Father will love him, and we will come to him and make our home with him. 24 He who does not love me will not obey my teaching. These words you hear are not my own; they belong to the Father who sent me.

²⁵ All this I have spoken while still with you. ²⁶ But the Counsellor, the Holy Spirit, whom the Father will send in my name, will teach you all things and will remind you of everything I have said to you. ²⁷ Peace I leave with you; my peace I give you. I do not give to you as the world gives. Do not let your hearts be troubled and do not be afraid.

²⁸ "You heard me say, 'I am going away and I am coming back to you.' If you loved me, you would be glad that I am going to the Father, for the Father is greater than I. ²⁹ I have told you now before it happens, so that when it does happen you will believe. ³⁰ I will not speak with you much longer, for the prince of this world is coming. He has no effect on me, ³¹ but the world must learn that I love the Father and that I do exactly what my Father has commanded me. Come now; let us leave.

The Vine and the Branches

15 "I am the true vine and my Father is the gardener. ² He cuts off every branch in me that bears no fruit, while every branch that does bear fruit he trims clean so that it will be even more fruitful. ³ You are already clean because of the word I have spoken to you. ⁴ Remain in me, and I will remain in you. No branch can bear fruit by itself; it must remain in the vine. Neither can you bear fruit unless you remain in me.

⁵ "I am the vine; you are the branches. If a man remains in me and I in him, he will bear much fruit; apart from me you can do nothing. ⁶ If anyone does not remain in me, he is like a branch that is thrown away and withers; such branches are picked up, thrown into the fire and burned. ⁷ If you remain in me and my words remain in you, ask whatever you wish, and it will be given you. ⁸ This is to my Father's glory, that you bear much fruit, showing yourselves to be my disciples.

⁹ "As the Father has loved me, so have I loved you. Now remain in my love. ¹⁰ If you obey my commands, you will remain in my love, just as I have obeyed my Father's commands and remain in his love. ¹¹ I have told you this so that

my joy may be in you and that your joy may be complete. ¹² My command is this: Love each other as I have loved you. ¹³ No one has greater love than the one who lays down his life for his friends. ¹⁴ You are my friends if you do what I command. ¹⁵ I no longer call you servants, because a servant does not know his master's business. Instead, I have called you friends, for everything that I learned from my Father I have made known to you. ¹⁶ You did not choose me, but I chose you to go and bear fruit—fruit that will last. Then the Father will give you whatever you ask in my name. ¹⁷ This is my command: Love each other.

The World Hates the Disciples

¹⁸ "If the world hates you, keep in mind that it hated me first. ¹⁹ If you belonged to the world, it would love you as its own. As it is, you do not belong to the world, but I have chosen you out of the world. That is why the world hates you. ²⁰ Remember the words I spoke to you: 'No servant is greater than his master.'^a If they persecuted me, they will persecute you also. If they obeyed my teaching, they will obey yours also. ²¹ They will treat you this way because of my name, for they do not know the one who sent me. ²² If I had not come and spoken to them, they would not be guilty of sin. Now, however, they have no excuse for their sin. ²³ He who hates me hates my Father as well. ²⁴ If I had not done among them what no one else did, they would not be guilty of sin. But now they have seen these miracles, and yet they have hated both me and my Father. ²⁵ But this is to fulfil what is written in their Law: 'They hated me without reason.'^b

²⁶ "When the Counsellor comes, whom I will send to you from the Father, the Spirit of truth who goes out from the Father, he will testify about me; ²⁷ but you also must testify, for you have been with me from the beginning.

16 "All this I have told you so that you will not go astray. ² They will put you out of the synagogue; in fact, a time is coming when anyone who kills you will think

^a 20 John 13:16   ^b 25 Psalm 35:19; 69:4

he is offering a service to God. ³ They will do such things because they have not known the Father or me. ⁴ I have told you this, so that when the time comes you will remember that I warned you. I did not tell you this at first because I was with you.

The Work of the Holy Spirit

⁵ "Now I am going to him who sent me, yet none of you even asks me, 'Where are you going?' ⁶ Because I have said these things, you are filled with grief. ⁷ But I tell you the truth: It is for your good that I am going away. Unless I go away, the Counsellor will not come to you; but if I go, I will send him to you. ⁸ When he comes, he will prove the world wrong about sin and righteousness and judgment: ⁹ about sin, because men do not believe in me; ¹⁰ about righteousness, because I am going to the Father, where you can see me no longer; ¹¹ and about judgment, because the prince of this world now stands condemned.

¹² "I have much more to say to you, more than you can now bear. ¹³ But when he, the Spirit of truth, comes, he will guide you into all truth. He will not speak on his own; he will speak only what he hears, and he will tell you what is yet to come. ¹⁴ He will bring glory to me by taking from what is mine and making it known to you. ¹⁵ All that belongs to the Father is mine. That is why I said the Spirit will take from what is mine and make it known to you.

¹⁶ "In a little while you will see me no more, and then after a little while you will see me."

The Disciples' Grief Will Turn to Joy

¹⁷ Some of his disciples said to one another, "What does he mean by saying, 'In a little while you will see me no more,' and 'Then after a little while you will see me,' and 'Because I am going to the Father'?" ¹⁸ They kept asking, "What does he mean by 'a little while'? We don't understand what he is saying."

¹⁹ Jesus saw that they wanted to ask him about this, so he said to them, "Are you asking one another what I meant when I said, 'In a little while you will see me no more,' and

'Then after a little while you will see me'? ²⁰ I tell you the truth, you will weep and mourn while the world rejoices. You will grieve, but your grief will turn to joy. ²¹ A woman giving birth to a child has pain because her time has come; but when her baby is born she forgets the anguish because of her joy that a child is born into the world. ²² So with you: Now is your time of grief, but I will see you again and you will rejoice, and no one will take away your joy. ²³ In that day you will no longer ask me anything. I tell you the truth, my Father will give you whatever you ask in my name. ²⁴ Until now you have not asked for anything in my name. Ask and you will receive, and your joy will be complete.

²⁵ "Though I have been speaking figuratively, a time is coming when I will no longer use this kind of language but will tell you plainly about my Father. ²⁶ In that day you will ask in my name. I am not saying that I will ask the Father on your behalf. ²⁷ No, the Father himself loves you because you have loved me and have believed that I came from God. ²⁸ I came from the Father and entered the world; now I am leaving the world and going back to the Father."

²⁹ Then Jesus' disciples said, "Now you are speaking clearly and without figures of speech. ³⁰ Now we can see that you know all things and that you do not even need to have anyone ask you questions. This makes us believe that you came from God."

³¹ "You believe at last!"ᵃ Jesus answered. ³² "But a time is coming, and has come, when you will be scattered, each to his own home. You will leave me all alone. Yet I am not alone, for my Father is with me.

³³ "I have told you these things, so that in me you may have peace. In this world you will have trouble. But take heart! I have overcome the world."

Jesus Prays for Himself

17 After Jesus said this, he looked toward heaven and prayed: "Father, the time has come. Glorify your Son, that your Son may glorify you. ² For you granted him authority over all men that he might give eternal life to all

ᵃ 31 Or "*Do you now believe?*"

43

those you have given to him. ³ Now this is eternal life: that they may know you, the only true God, and Jesus Christ, whom you have sent. ⁴ I have brought you glory on earth by completing the work you gave me to do. ⁵ And now, Father, glorify me in your presence with the glory I had with you before the world began.

Jesus Prays for His Disciples

⁶ "I have revealed you to those whom you gave me out of the world. They were yours; you gave them to me and they have obeyed your word. ⁷ Now they know that everything you have given me comes from you. ⁸ For I gave them the words you gave me and they accepted them. They knew with certainty that I came from you, and they believed that you sent me. ⁹ I pray for them. I am not praying for the world, but for those you have given me, for they are yours. ¹⁰ All I have is yours, and all you have is mine. And glory has come to me through them. ¹¹ I will remain in the world no longer, but they are still in the world, and I am coming to you. Holy Father, protect them by the power of your name—the name you gave me—so that they may be one as we are one. ¹² While I was with them, I protected them and kept them safe by that name you gave me. None has been lost except the child of hell so that Scripture would be fulfilled.

¹³ "I am coming to you now, but I say these things while I am still in the world, so that they may have the full measure of my joy within them. ¹⁴ I have given them your word and the world has hated them, for they are not of the world any more than I am of the world. ¹⁵ My prayer is not that you take them out of the world but that you protect them from the evil one. ¹⁶ They are not of the world, even as I am not of it. ¹⁷ Sanctify*ᵃ* them by the truth; your word is truth. ¹⁸ As you sent me into the world, I have sent them into the world. ¹⁹ For them I sanctify*ᵃ* myself, that they too may be truly sanctified.*ᵃ*

ᵃ 17, 19 Greek *hagiazo* (*set apart for sacred use* or *make holy*)

Jesus Prays for All Believers

²⁰ "My prayer is not for them alone. I pray also for those who will believe in me through their message, ²¹ that all of them may be one, Father, just as you are in me and I am in you. May they also be in us so that the world may believe that you have sent me. ²² I have given them the glory that you gave me, that they may be one as we are one: ²³ I in them and you in me. May they be brought to complete unity to let the world know that you sent me and have loved them even as you have loved me.

²⁴ "Father, I want those you have given me to be with me where I am, and to see my glory, the glory you have given me because you loved me before the creation of the world.

²⁵ "Righteous Father, though the world does not know you, I know you, and they know that you have sent me. ²⁶ I have revealed you*ᵇ* to them, and will continue to make you known in order that the love you have for me may be theirs and that I myself may be in them."

Jesus Arrested

18 When he had finished praying, Jesus left with his disciples and crossed the Kidron Valley. On the other side there was an olive grove, and he and his disciples went into it.

² Now Judas, who betrayed him, knew the place, because Jesus had often met there with his disciples. ³ So Judas came to the grove, guiding a detachment of soldiers and some officials from the chief priests and Pharisees. They were carrying torches, lanterns and weapons.

⁴ Jesus, knowing all that was going to happen to him, went out and asked them, "Who is it you want?"

⁵ "Jesus of Nazareth," they replied.

"I am he," Jesus said. (And Judas the traitor was standing there with them.) ⁶ When Jesus said, "I am he," they drew back and fell to the ground.

⁷ Again he asked them, "Who is it you want?"

And they said, "Jesus of Nazareth."

ᵇ 26 Or have made your name known

8 "I told you that I am he," Jesus answered. "If you are looking for me, then let these men go." 9 This happened so that the words he had spoken would be fulfilled: "I have not lost one of those you gave me."*a*

10 Then Simon Peter, who had a sword, drew it and struck the high priest's servant, cutting off his right ear. (The servant's name was Malchus.)

11 Jesus commanded Peter, "Put your sword away! Shall I not drink the cup the Father has given me?"

Jesus Taken to Annas

12 Then the detachment of soldiers with its commander and the Jewish officials arrested Jesus. They bound him 13 and brought him first to Annas, who was the father-in-law of Caiaphas, the high priest that year. 14 Caiaphas was the one who had advised the Jews that it would be good if one man died for the people.

Peter's First Denial

15 Simon Peter and another disciple were following Jesus. Because this disciple was known to the high priest, he went with Jesus into the high priest's courtyard, 16 but Peter had to wait outside at the door. The other disciple, who was known to the high priest, came back, spoke to the girl on duty there, and brought Peter in.

17 "Surely you are not another of this man's disciples?" the girl at the door asked Peter.

He replied, "I am not."

18 It was cold, and the servants and officials stood around a fire they had made to keep warm. Peter also was standing with them, warming himself.

The High Priest Questions Jesus

19 Meanwhile, the high priest questioned Jesus about his disciples and his teaching.

20 "I have spoken openly to the world," Jesus replied. "I always taught in synagogues or at the temple, where all the Jews come together. I said nothing in secret. 21 Why ques-

a 9 John 6:39

tion me? Ask those who heard me. Surely they know what I said."

²² When Jesus had said this, one of the officials near by struck him in the face. "Is that any way to answer the high priest?" he demanded.

²³ "If I said something wrong," Jesus replied, "speak up about it. But if I spoke the truth, why did you hit me?" ²⁴ Then Annas sent him, still bound, to Caiaphas, the high priest.*b*

Peter's Second and Third Denials

²⁵ As Simon Peter stood warming himself, he was asked, "Surely you are not another of his disciples?"

He denied it, saying, "I am not."

²⁶ One of the high priest's servants, a relative of the man whose ear Peter had cut off, challenged him, "Didn't I see you with him in the olive grove?" ²⁷ Again Peter denied it, and at that moment a cock began to crow.

Jesus Before Pilate

²⁸ Then the Jews led Jesus from Caiaphas to the palace of the Roman governor. By now it was early morning, and to avoid ceremonial uncleanness the Jews did not enter the palace; they wanted to be able to eat the Passover. ²⁹ So Pilate came out to them and asked, "What charges are you bringing against this man?"

³⁰ "If he were not a criminal," they replied, "we would not have handed him over to you."

³¹ Pilate said, "Take him yourselves and judge him by your own law."

"But we have no right to execute anyone," the Jews objected. ³² This happened so that the words Jesus had spoken indicating the kind of death he was going to die would be fulfilled.

³³ Pilate then went back inside the palace, summoned Jesus, and asked him, "Are you the king of the Jews?"

³⁴ "Is that your own idea," Jesus asked, "or did others talk to you about me?"

b 24 Or (*Now Annas had sent . . . the high priest*)

³⁵ "Do you think I am a Jew?" Pilate replied. "It was your people and your chief priests who handed you over to me. What is it you have done?"

³⁶ Jesus said, "My kingdom is not of this world. If it were, my servants would fight to prevent my arrest by the Jews. But now my kingdom is from another place."

³⁷ "You are a king, then!" said Pilate.

Jesus answered, "You are right in saying I am a king. In fact, for this reason I was born, and for this I came into the world, to testify to the truth. Everyone on the side of truth listens to me."

³⁸ "What is truth?" Pilate asked. With this he went out again to the Jews and said, "I find no basis for a charge against him. ³⁹ But it is your custom for me to release to you one prisoner at the time of the Passover. Do you want me to release 'the king of the Jews'?"

⁴⁰ They shouted back, "No, not him! Give us Barabbas!" Now Barabbas had taken part in a rebellion.

Jesus Sentenced to be Crucified

19 Then Pilate took Jesus and had him flogged. ² The soldiers twisted together a crown of thorns and put it on his head. They clothed him in a purple robe ³ and went up to him again and again, saying, "Hail, O king of the Jews!" And they struck him in the face.

⁴ Once more Pilate came out and said to the Jews, "Look, I am bringing him out to you to let you know that I find no basis for a charge against him." ⁵ When Jesus came out wearing the crown of thorns and the purple robe, Pilate said to them, "Here is the man!"

⁶ As soon as the chief priests and their officials saw him, they shouted, "Crucify! Crucify!"

But Pilate answered, "You take him and crucify him. As for me, I find no basis for a charge against him."

⁷ The Jews insisted, "We have a law, and according to that law he must die, because he claimed to be the Son of God."

⁸ When Pilate heard this, he was even more afraid, ⁹ and he went back inside the palace. "Where do you come from?"

he asked Jesus, but Jesus gave him no answer. [10] "Do you refuse to speak to me?" Pilate said. "Don't you realize I have power either to free you or to crucify you?"

[11] Jesus answered, "You have no power over me that was not given to you from above. Therefore the one who handed me over to you is guilty of a greater sin."

[12] From then on, Pilate tried to set Jesus free, but the Jews kept shouting, "If you let this man go, you are no friend of Caesar. Anyone who claims to be a king opposes Caesar."

[13] When Pilate heard this, he brought Jesus out and sat down on the judge's seat at a place known as The Stone Pavement (which in Aramaic is Gabbatha). [14] It was the day of Preparation of Passover Week, about the sixth hour.

"Here is your king," Pilate said to the Jews.

[15] But they shouted, "Take him away! Take him away! Crucify him!"

"Shall I crucify your king?" Pilate asked.

"We have no king but Caesar," the chief priests answered.

[16] Finally Pilate handed him over to them to be crucified.

The Crucifixion

So the soldiers took charge of Jesus. [17] Carrying his own cross, he went out to The Place of the Skull (which in Aramaic is called Golgotha). [18] Here they crucified him, and with him two others—one on either side and Jesus in the middle.

[19] Pilate had a notice prepared and fastened to the cross. It read, JESUS OF NAZARETH, THE KING OF THE JEWS. [20] Many of the Jews read this sign, for the place where Jesus was crucified was near the city, and the sign was written in Aramaic, Latin and Greek. [21] The chief priests of the Jews protested to Pilate, "Do not write 'The King of the Jews,' but that this man claimed to be king of the Jews."

[22] Pilate answered, "What I have written, I have written."

[23] When the soldiers crucified Jesus, they took his clothes, dividing them into four shares, one for each of them, with the undergarment remaining. This garment was seamless, woven in one piece from top to bottom.

[24] "Let's not tear it," they said to one another. "Let's decide by lot who will get it."

This happened that the scripture might be fulfilled which said,

> "They divided my garments among themselves
> and cast lots for my clothing."[a]

So this is what the soldiers did.

[25] Near the cross of Jesus stood his mother, his mother's sister, Mary the wife of Clopas, and Mary of Magdala. [26] When Jesus saw his mother there, and the disciple whom he loved standing near by, he said to his mother, "Here is[b] your son," [27] and to the disciple, "Here is your mother." From that time on, this disciple took her into his home.

The Death of Jesus

[28] Later, knowing that all was now completed, and so that the scripture would be fulfilled, Jesus said, "I am thirsty." [29] A jar of wine vinegar was there, so they soaked a sponge in it, put the sponge on a stalk of the hyssop plant, and lifted it to Jesus' lips. [30] When he had received the drink, Jesus said, "It is finished." With that, he bowed his head and gave up his life.

[31] Now it was the day of Preparation, and the next day was to be a special Sabbath. Because the Jews did not want the bodies left on the crosses during the Sabbath, they asked Pilate to have the legs broken and the bodies taken down. [32] The soldiers therefore came and broke the legs of the first man who had been crucified with Jesus, and then those of the other. [33] But when they came to Jesus and found that he was already dead, they did not break his legs. [34] Instead, one of the soldiers pierced Jesus' side with a spear, bringing a sudden flow of blood and water. [35] The man who saw it has given testimony, and his testimony is true. He knows that he tells the truth, and he testifies so that you also may have faith. [36] These things happened so that the scripture would be fulfilled, "Not one of his bones will be broken."[c] [37] and,

a 24 Psalm 22:18
b 26 Greek *"Woman, here is . . ."* (a polite form of address)
c 36 Exodus 12:46; Num. 9:12; Psalm 34:20

as another scripture says, "They will look on the one they
have pierced."[d]

The Burial of Jesus

[38] Later, Joseph of Arimathea asked Pilate for the body
of Jesus. Now Joseph was a disciple of Jesus, but secretly
because he feared the Jews. With Pilate's permission, he
came and took the body. [39] He was accompanied by
Nicodemus, the man who earlier had visited Jesus at night.
Nicodemus brought a mixture of myrrh and aloes, about
seventy-five pounds. [40] Taking Jesus' body, the two of them
wrapped it, with the spices, in strips of linen. This was in
accordance with Jewish burial customs. [41] At the place
where Jesus was crucified, there was a garden, and in the
garden a new tomb, in which no one had ever been laid.
[42] Because it was the Jewish day of Preparation and since
the tomb was near by, they laid Jesus there.

The Empty Tomb

20 Early on the first day of the week, while it was still
dark, Mary of Magdala went to the tomb and saw that
the stone had been removed from the entrance. [2] So she
came running to Simon Peter and the other disciple, the
one Jesus loved, and said, "They have taken the Lord out
of the tomb, and we don't know where they have put
him!"

[3] So Peter and the other disciple started for the tomb.
[4] Both were running, but the other disciple outran Peter,
and reached the tomb first. [5] He bent over and looked in at
the strips of linen lying there but did not go in. [6] Then Simon
Peter, who was behind him, arrived and went into the tomb.
He saw the strips of linen lying there, [7] as well as the burial
cloth that had been around Jesus' head. The cloth was
folded up by itself, separate from the linen. [8] Finally the
other disciple, who had reached the tomb first, also went
inside. He saw and believed. [9] (They still did not understand
from Scripture that Jesus had to rise from the dead.)

[d] 37 Zech. 12:10

Jesus Appears to Mary of Magdala

¹⁰ Then the disciples went back to their homes, ¹¹ but Mary stood outside the tomb crying. As she wept, she bent over to look into the tomb ¹² and saw two angels in white, seated where Jesus' body had been, one at the head and the other at the foot.

¹³ They asked her, "Woman, why are you crying?"

"They have taken my Lord away," she said, "and I don't know where they have put him." ¹⁴ At this, she turned around and saw Jesus standing there, but she did not realize that it was Jesus.

¹⁵ "Woman," he said, "why are you crying? Who is it you are looking for?"

Thinking he was the gardener, she said, "Sir, if you have carried him away, tell me where you have put him, and I will get him."

¹⁶ Jesus said to her, "Mary."

She turned toward him and cried out in Aramaic, "Rabboni!" (which means Teacher).

¹⁷ Jesus said, "Do not hold on to me, for I have not yet returned to the Father. Go instead to my brothers and tell them, 'I am returning to my Father and your Father, to my God and your God.'" ¹⁸ Mary of Magdala went to the disciples with the news that she had seen the Lord and that he had told her this.

Jesus Appears to His Disciples

¹⁹ On the evening of that first day of the week, when the disciples were together, with the doors locked for fear of the Jews, Jesus came and stood among them and said, "Peace be with you!" ²⁰ After he said this, he showed them his hands and side. The disciples were overjoyed when they saw the Lord.

²¹ Again Jesus said, "Peace be with you! As the Father has sent me, I am sending you." ²² And with that he breathed on them and said, "Receive the Holy Spirit. ²³ If you forgive anyone his sins, they are forgiven; if you do not forgive them, they are not forgiven."

Jesus Appears to Thomas

²⁴ Now Thomas (called Didymus), one of the Twelve, was not with the disciples when Jesus came. ²⁵ When the other disciples told him that they had seen the Lord, he declared, "Unless I see the nail marks in his hands and put my finger where the nails were, and put my hand into his side, I will not believe it."

²⁶ A week later his disciples were in the house again, and Thomas was with them. Though the doors were locked, Jesus came and stood among them, and said, "Peace be with you!" ²⁷ Then he said to Thomas, "Put your finger here; see my hands. Reach out your hand and put it into my side. Stop doubting and believe."

²⁸ Thomas answered, "My Lord and my God!"

²⁹ Then Jesus told him, "Because you have seen me, you have believed; blessed are those who have not seen and yet have believed."

³⁰ Jesus did many other miraculous signs in the presence of his disciples, which are not recorded in this book. ³¹ But these are written that you may believe*ᵃ* that Jesus is the Christ, the Son of God, and that by believing you may have life in his name.

Jesus and the Miraculous Catch of Fish

21 Afterwards Jesus appeared again to his disciples by the Sea of Tiberias. It happened this way: ² Simon Peter, Thomas (called Didymus), Nathanael from Cana in Galilee, the sons of Zebedee, and two other disciples were together. ³ "I'm going out to fish," Simon Peter told them, and they said, "We'll go with you." So they went out and got into the boat, but that night they caught nothing.

⁴ Early in the morning, Jesus stood on the shore, but the disciples did not realize that it was Jesus.

⁵ He called out to them, "Friends, haven't you caught any fish?"

"No," they answered.

ᵃ 31 Or *that you may continue to believe* ...

⁶ He said, "Throw your net on the right side of the boat and you will find some." When they did, they were unable to haul the net in because of the large number of fish.

⁷ Then the disciple whom Jesus loved said to Peter, "It is the Lord!" As soon as Simon Peter heard him say, "It is the Lord," he wrapped his outer garment around him (for he had taken it off) and jumped into the water. ⁸ The other disciples followed in the boat, towing the net full of fish, for they were not far from shore, about a hundred yards. ⁹ When they landed, they saw a fire of burning coals there with fish on it, and some bread.

¹⁰ Jesus said to them, "Bring some of the fish you have just caught."

¹¹ Simon Peter climbed aboard and dragged the net ashore. It was full of large fish, 153, but even with so many the net was not torn. ¹² Jesus said to them, "Come and have breakfast." None of the disciples dared ask him, "Who are you?" They knew it was the Lord. ¹³ Jesus came, took the bread and gave it to them, and did the same with the fish. ¹⁴ This was now the third time Jesus appeared to his disciples after he was raised from the dead.

Jesus Reinstates Peter

¹⁵ When they had finished eating, Jesus said to Simon Peter, "Simon son of John, do you truly love me more than these?"

"Yes, Lord," he said, "you know that I love you."

Jesus said, "Feed my lambs."

¹⁶ Again Jesus said, "Simon son of John, do you truly love me?"

He answered, "Yes, Lord, you know that I love you."

Jesus said, "Take care of my sheep."

¹⁷ The third time he said to him, "Simon son of John, do you love me?"

Peter was hurt because Jesus asked him the third time, "Do you love me?" He said, "Lord, you know all things; you know that I love you."

Jesus said, "Feed my sheep. ¹⁸ I tell you the truth, when you were younger you dressed yourself and went where you wanted; but when you are old you will stretch out your hands, and someone else will dress you and lead you where you do not want to go." [19] Jesus said this to indicate the kind of death by which Peter would glorify God. Then he said to him, "Follow me!"

[20] Peter turned and saw that the disciple whom Jesus loved was following them. (This was the one who had leaned back against Jesus at the supper and had said, "Lord, who is going to betray you?") [21] When Peter saw him, he asked, "Lord, what about him?"

[22] Jesus answered, "If I want him to remain alive until I return, what is that to you? You must follow me." [23] Because of this, the rumour spread among the brothers that this disciple would not die. But Jesus did not say that he would not die; he only said, "If I want him to remain alive until I return, what is that to you?"

[24] This is the disciple who testifies to these things and who wrote them down. We know that his testimony is true.

[25] Jesus did many other things as well. If every one of them were written down, I suppose that even the whole world would not have room for the books that would be written.